Published by
Southwestern Press
P.O. Box 4297
Carlsbad, CA 92018
(760) 434-8858
www.southwesternpress.com

W9-BKH-180

7/03

WITHDRAWN

Copyright © 1992 by Southwestern Press

Todos los derechos literarios son reservados bajo las convenciones Pan American e Internacional.

Ninguna porción de este libro puede ser reproducido o transmitido de ninguna forma, ya sea electrónica o mecanicamente, incluyendo fotocopias, grabaciones por ningun sistema de almacenamiento o recuperación, sin el permiso por escrito del dueño de los derechos literarios, exceptuando las frases o palabras repetidas incluídas en los repasos de palabras.

No part of this book may be reproduced or transmitted in any form or by any means, electronic or mechanical, including photocopying, recording or by any information storage and retrieval system, without the written permission of the copyright owner, except for brief quotations embodied in review.

Printed in the United States of America.

ISBN 0-923176-10-1

I.C.C. LIBRARY

INTRODUCCION

¿Cuál es la manera más fácil y rápida para
comunicarse con un patrón o empleador que habla
Inglés?

¡INGLES EN EL TRABAJO! Esta guía de palabras fác.
y rápida está especialmente diseñada para ofrecer a
trabajadores de habla hispana la habilidad de
comunicarse inmediatamente con el patrón o
empleador.

Esta guía completa y concisa está escrita para
ayudarle a que encuentre un trabajo mejor y aumente
al máximo su entendimiento en total, especialmente
en el ramo de la construcción, jardinería y servicio
doméstico.

Cada frase u oración es presentada en Inglés
Español y está fonéticamente deletreada para
asegurar su pronunciación.

¡No necesita tener conocimientos anteriores del
idioma Inglés!

TABLE DE CONTENIDO

WITHDRAWN

Parte I

PALABRAS Y FRASES COMUNES

PALABRAS Y FRASES COMUNES

DINERO **MONEY**
món-i

¿CUÁNTO?	How much? jau móch
CHEQUE	check chék
EFECTIVO	cash kásh
GIRO POSTAL	money order món-i ór-dr
MI CHEQUE ESTÁ INCORRECTO.	My check is wrong. mai chék is rong.
¿NECESITAS DINERO?	Do you need money? du yu nid món-i
¿NECESITAS UN ANTICIPO?	Do you need an advance? du yu nid en ad-vaans
NECESITO MAS DINERO.	I need more money. ai nid mor món-i.
NECESITO UN ADELANTO.	I need an advance. ai nid en ad-váns
POR FAVOR PAGUEME EN EFECTIVO.	Please pay me in cash. pliz pei mi en kásh

INGLES EN
EL TRABAJO

¿QUE TANTO PAGA?	How much is the pay? jau móch is da pei
¿SE ME PAGARÁ POR MIS VACACIONES?	Do I get vacation pay? du ai get vei-kéi-shen pei
TENGO CUENTA DE BANCO.	I have a bank account. ai jav a bánk a-káunt
UD. ME PUEDE PAGARME CON CHEQUE.	You may pay me with a check. ju mei pei mi uíz a chék
YO NECESITO DINERO.	I need money. ai nid món-i.
PAGO _____ LA HORA.	I pay _____ an hour. ai pei _____ an áuer.
YO COBRO _____ LA HORA.	I charge _____ an hour. ai chardch _____ en áuer.
EL DÍA	a day
LA SEMANA	a week
EL MES	a month
MÁS EL CUARTO Y COMIDA	plus room and board

PALABRAS Y FRASES COMUNES

$5.00	five dollars faif dó-lors
$5.25	five twenty-five faif tuénti-faif
$5.50	five fifty faif fífti
$5.75	five seventy-five faif sé-ven-ti-faif
$6.00	six dollars siks dó-lars
$30.00	thirty dollars zér-ti dó-lars
$40.00	forty dollars fór-ti dó-lars
$45.00	forty-five dollars fór-ti-faif dó-lars
$100.00	one hundred dollars uón jón-dred dó-lars
$102.00	one hundred and two dollars uán jón-dred and tu dó-lars

INGLES EN
EL TRABAJO

$140.00	one hundred and forty dollars uán jón-dred and fór-ti dó-lars
$200.00	two hundred dollars tu jón-dred dó-lars
$300.00	three hundred dollars zri jón-dred dó-lars
$400.00	four hundred dollars for jón-dred dó-lars
$500.00	five hundred dollars faif jón-dred dó-lars
$600.00	six hundred dollars sik jón-dred dó-lars
$700.00	seven hundred dollars sé-ven jón-dred dó-lars
$800.00	eight hundred dollars eit jón-dred dó-lars
$900.00	nine hundred dollars náin jón-dred dó-lars
$1000.00	one thousand dollars uán záu-sand dó-lars

PALABRAS Y FRASES COMUNES

¿CUÁNDO ME PAGARÁ?	When will you pay me?
	juen juil yu pei me
SE PAGA _____ .	I pay every _____ .
	ai pei év-ri _____ .
TE PAGARÉ EL _____ .	I will pay you on _____ .
	ai juil pei yu an _____ .
DOMINGO	Sunday
	són-dei
LUNES	Monday
	món-dei
MARTES	Tuesday
	tús-dei
MIÉRCOLES	Wednesday
	uéns-dei
JUEVES	Thursday
	zérs-dei
VIERNES	Friday
	frái-dei
SÁBADO	Saturday
	sát-er-dei

THIS ITEM CHARGED TO

Patron: MENCHY SANCHEZ
Patron Barcod

[barcode]
2 0 1 6 1 0 0 1 2 0 9 9 5

Due Date: 7/22/2005 04:00 PM

Title: English on the job = Ingles en el
trabajo
Author:
Call Number: PE1131 .E634 1992

1

Item Barcode:

[barcode]
A 1 2 9 0 1 6 5 0 6 0

THINK JOHN WOOD FIRST

INGLES EN
EL TRABAJO

COLORES	**COLORS** cá-lors
AMARILLO	yellow yé-lou
AZUL	blue blú
BLANCO	white uáit
CAFÉ	brown bráun
CLARO	light lait
GRIS	gray grei
MORADO	purple pér-pel
NEGRO	black blák
ANARANJADO	orange ór-anch
OSCURO	dark dáark
ROJO	red red
ROSADO	pink pínk
VERDE	green gríin

PALABRAS Y FRASES COMUNES

EXPRESIONES DEL TIEMPO

¿A QUÉ HORA DEBO PRESENTARME?	What time should I be here? juat taim chúud ai bi jir
¿A QUÉ HORA DEBO PARAR DE TRABAJAR?	What time will I stop work? juat taim juil ai stop uórk
¿A QUÉ HORA ME PUEDO IR?	What time may I leave? juat taim mei ai liv
¿CUÁLES SON LAS HORAS QUE DEBERÉ TRABAJAR?	What are the hours I will work? juat ar da auers ai juil uórk
EMPIEZA A TRABAJAR A LA(S) _____ .	Start work at _____ . stáart uórk at _____
ESTE AQUÍ A LA(S) _____ .	Be here at _____ . bi jir at _____
PARA A LA(S) _____ .	Quit at _____ . kuit at _____
¿QUÉ HORA ES?	What time is it? juat taim is it
TÚ PUEDES IR A LA(S) _____ .	You may leave at _____ . yu mei liv at _____
YO ESTARÉ AQUÍ A _____ .	I will be here at _____ . ai juil bi jir at _____ _

INGLES EN
EL TRABAJO

LA HORA	TIME taim
1:00	one o'clock uán o-klok
1:15	one fifteen uán fef-tin
1:30	one thirty uán zér-ti
1:45	one forty-five uán fór-ti-faif
2:00	two o'clock tu o-klok
3:00	three o'clock zrí o-klok
4:00	four o'clock for o'klok
5:00	five o'clock faif o-klok
6:00	six o'clock siks o-klok
7:00	seven o'clock sé-ven o-klok

PALABRAS Y FRASES COMUNES

8:00	eight o'clock éit o-klok
9:00	nine o'clock nain o-klok
10:00	ten o'clock ten o-klok
11:00	eleven o'clock i-lé-ven o-klok
12:00	twelve o'clock tuelf o-klok

EXPRESIONES DEL TIEMPO

¿CUÁNDO ES MI DÍA LIBRE?	When is my day off? juen is mai dei af
¿CUÁNDO EMPIEZO A TRABAJAR?	When do I start work? juen du ai stáart uórk
YO ESTARÉ AQUÍ EL (DÍA).	I will be here (day). ai juil bi jir (dei)
DESCANSARÁS LOS (DÍA).	You will have (day) off. yu juil jav (dei) af
VAS A TRABAJAR _____ (horas, dias, meses)	You will work _____ . (hours, days, months) yu jui uórk _____ . (áuers, deis, monz)
DOMINGO	Sunday són-dei
LUNES	Monday món-dei
MARTES	Tuesday tús-dei
MIÉRCOLES	Wednesday uéns-dei
JUEVES	Thursday zérs-dei

PALABRAS Y FRASES COMUNES

VIERNES	Friday
	frái-dei
SÁBADO	Saturday
	sát-er-dei

INGLES EN
EL TRABAJO

AÑO	year jír
AYER	yesterday yés-ter-dei
DÍA	day dei
ESTE DÍA	today tu-déi
ESTA NOCHE	tonight tu-náit
HORA	hour áuer
HOY	today tu-déi
MAÑANA	morning mór-ning
MAÑANA	tomorrow tu-mór-ou
MEDIODÍA	noon núun
MEDIANOCHE	midnight míd-nait

PALABRAS Y FRASES COMUNES

MES	month monz
MINUTO	minute mín-it
NOCHE	night náit
SEMANA	week uuík
SEMANA QUE ENTRA	next week nekst úuik
TARDE	afternoon af-ter-núun

INGLES EN
EL TRABAJO

LOS DÍAS

THE DAYS
da deiz

DOMINGO

Sunday
són-dei

LUNES

Monday
món-dei

MARTES

Tuesday
tús-dei

MIÉRCOLES

Wednesday
uéns-dei

JUEVES

Thursday
zérs-dei

VIERNES

Friday
frái-dei

SÁBADO

Saturday
sát-er-dei

INGLES PARA
UN EMPLEO MEJOR

LOS MESES   **THE MONTHS**
                                 da monz

ENERO	**January** chán-u-eri
FEBRERO	**February** féb-ru-eri
MARZO	**March** march
ABRIL	**April** éi-pril
MAYO	**May** mei
JUNIO	**June** chun
JULIO	**July** chu-lái
AGOSTO	**August** ó-gost
SEPTIEMBRE	**September** sep-tém-ber
OCTUBRE	**October** ak-tó-ber
NOVIEMBRE	**November** no-vém-ber
DICIEMBRE	**December** di-cém-ber

PALABRAS Y FRASES COMUNES

LOS NÚMEROS

THE NUMBERS
da nam-bers

0	zero	zíro
1	one	uán
2	two	tu
3	three	zrí
4	four	for
5	five	fáif
6	six	siks
7	seven	sé-ven
8	eight	éit
9	nine	nain
10	ten	ten

INGLES EN
EL TRABAJO

11	eleven i-lé-ven
12	twelve tuelf
13	thirteen zér-tin
14	fourteen fór-tin
15	fifteen féf-tin
16	sixteen síks-tin
17	seventeen sé-ven-tin
18	eighteen éit-tin
19	nineteen náin-tin
20	twenty túen-ti
21	twenty-one tuen-ti-uán

PALABRAS Y FRASES COMUNES

30	thirty zér-ti
40	forty fór-ti
50	fifty féf-ti
60	sixty síks-ti
70	seventy sé-ven-ti
80	eighty éit-ti
90	ninty náin-ti
100	one hundred uán jón-dred
1000	one thousand uán záu-sand

INGLES EN
EL TRABAJO

PRIMERO	first ferst
SEGUNDO	second sék-and
TERCERO	third zérd
CUARTO	fourth fórz
QUINTO	fifth fífz
SEXTO	sixth sikz
SÉPTIMO	seventh sé-venz
OCTAVO	eighth éitz
NOVENO	ninth náinz
DÉCIMO	tenth tenz

PALABRAS Y FRASES COMUNES

BUSCANDO TRABAJO

ESTOY BUSCANDO TRABAJO.
  I'm looking for a job.
  aim lúk-ing for a chab

ESTOY BUSCANDO UN POCO DE TRABAJO.
  I'm looking for a little work.
  aim lúk-ing for a lit-tl uórk

ESTOY BUSCANDO UN TRABAJO DE MEDIO TIEMPO.
  I'm looking for a part-time job.
  aim lúk-ing for a páart taim chab

ESTOY BUSCANDO UN TRABAJO DE TIEMPO COMPLETO.
  I'm looking for a full time job.
  aim lúk-ing for a fúl taim chab

¿ME PUEDE DAR UNA SOLICITUD DE EMPLEO?
  May I have an application?
  mei ai jav en ap-la-kéi-shen

POR FAVOR HABLE DESPACIO MI INGLÉS NO ES MUY BUENO.
  Please speak slowly my English is not very good.
  pliz spik slo-li mai Ing-lesh iz not vér-i gud

PUEDO TRABAJAR NOCHES/FINES DE SEMANA.
  I can work nights / weekends.
  ai can uórk naitz / úik-endz

¿HAY ALGUNA CLASE DE PRESTACIONES?
  Are there benefits?
  ar dér bén-i-fitz

INGLES PARA
UN EMPLEO MEJOR

POR FAVOR DEJE UN MENSAJE CON MI...
Please leave a message with my...
pliz liv a més-ich úid mai...

...MI ABUELA/ABUELO.
grandmother/grandfather.
gránd-mod-er/gránd-faa-der

...AMIGA(O).
friend.
frénd

...ESPOSA/ESPOSO.
wife/husband.
úaif/jós-band

...HERMANA/HERMANO.
sister/brother.
sis-ter/bród-er

...HIJA/HIJO.
daughter/son.
dó-ter/són

...MADRE/PADRE.
mother/father.
mód-er/fáa-der

...TÍA/TÍO.
aunt/uncle.
áan/ón-klt

PALABRAS Y FRASES COMUNES

RECIENTEMENTE TRABAJÉ EN UN(A)...
Recently I worked at a...
rí-senti-li ai uórkd at a...

...CASA EN ESTA AREA.
house in the area.
aus en da é-ri-a

...ESCUELA.
school
skúul

...HOSPITAL.
hospital.
jós-pi-tal

...HOTEL.
hotel.
jó-tel

...SITIO DE CONSTRUCCIÓN.
construction site.
con-stroc-shon sait

...TIENDA DE ABARROTES.
grocery store.
gróu-se-ri stór

INGLES EN
EL TRABAJO

TENGO EXPERIENCIA EN...
I have experience in...
ai jav eks-pír-i-ens en...

...AGRICULTURA.
farming.
áarm-ing

...ALBAÑILERÍA.
masonry.
mei-son-ri

...CARPINTERÍA.
carpentry.
cár-pen-tri

...COCINERO.
cooking.
kúk-ing

...CONSTRUCCIÓN.
construction.
con-stroc-shon

...COSTURA.
sewing.
sóu-ing

...CUIDADO DE NIÑOS.
childcare.
cháild-ker

PALABRAS Y FRASES COMUNES

...JARDINERÍA
gardening.
gáar-dn-ing

...LAVADO Y PLANCHADO DE ROPA.
washing and ironing.
uásh-ing and ai-er-ning

...LIMPIEZA Y MANTENIMIENTO DE EDIFICIOS.
janitorial.
yán-e-tor-i-el

...MANTENIMIENTO.
maintenance.
méin-te-nans

...MAQUINARIA BÁSICA.
basic machinery.
béi-sik ma-shín-er-i

...MECÁNICA DE AUTOMÓVILES.
auto mechanics.
o-to mi-kan-iks

...PINTURA.
painting.
peín-ting

...PLOMERÍA.
plumbing.
plóm-ing

INGLES EN
EL TRABAJO

...QUEHACERES DOMÉSTICOS.
housecleaning.
jáus-kliin-ing

...RESTAURANTES.
restaurants.
rés-to-rants

PALABRAS Y FRASES COMUNES

¿CUÁLES SON LAS HORAS QUE DEBERÉ TRABAJAR?
What are the hours I will work?
juat ar da auers ai uil uórk

¿CUÁNDO ES MI DÍA LIBRE?
When is my day off?
juen iz mai dei af

¿CUÁNDO SON MIS VACACIONES?
When is my vacation?
juen iz mai vei--kéi-shen

TENGO / NO TENGO TARJETA DE SEGURO SOCIAL.
I have / don't have my social security card.
ai jav / dount jav mai só-shial se-kiur-it-i kard

TENGO / NO TENGO TARJETA VERDE.
I have / don't have my green card.
ai jav / dount jav mai grin kard

TENGO TELÉFONO. MI NÚMERO ES ...
I have a telephone. The number is ...
ai jav a tél-e-fon da nám-ber iz

YO LE PUEDE PROPORCIONAR REFERENCIAS DE PERSONAS CON LAS QUE HE TRABAJADO EN ESTA AREA.
I can give you references from people I have worked for in this area.
ai can guív yu réf-fren-sez fróm píi-pl ai jav uórked for en dis é-ri-a

INGLES EN
EL TRABAJO

YO PUEDO ESCRIBIR.
> I can write.
> ai kan rait

YO PUEDO HABLAR UN POCO DE INGLÉS.
> I speak a little English.
> ai spik a lit-tl Ing-lesh

YO PUEDO LEER.
> I can read.
> ai kan ríid

YO VENGO POR AQUÍ CADA: (DÍA, SEMANA, MES.)
> I come by here every: (day, week, month.)
> ai kóm bai jir év-ri dei, uuík, monz

TENGO / NO TENGO DIRECCIÓN PARA RECIBIR CORREO.
> I have / do not have a mailing address.
> ai jav / du nót jav a méil-ing a-drés

PALABRAS Y FRASES COMUNES

PALABRAS Y FRASES

ABAJO	below bi-lóu
ABAJO	down dáun
ABIERTO	open óu-pn
ABRIR	open óu-pn
ADENTRO	inside in-sáid
AHORA	now náu
AL TRAVÉS	across a-krós
ALLÍ	there dér
ALMUERZO	lunch lónch
ALTO	high, tall hai, tal
ANCHO	wide uáid

INGLES EN
EL TRABAJO

ANTES	before bi-fór
APAGAR	turn off tern af
APILAR	stack stáck
¡APÚRATE!	Hurry up! jú-ri ap
AQUÍ	here jir
ARRIBA	up above ap a-baf
ATRÁS	back bák
AYUDA/AYUDAR	help jélp
BAJO	short shórt
BASTANTE	enough i-nóf
BEBER	drink drínk

PALABRAS Y FRASES COMUNES

BIEN	right ráit
BUENO	good gúd
BUSCA/BUSCAR	look for
BUSCA/BUSCAR	search sérch
CAFÉ	coffee kóf-i
CALENTAR	warm uórm
CALIENTE	hot jat
CARRO	car káar
CENA	dinner dín-er
CERCA DE	near nier
CERRADO	closed klóuzd

INGLES EN
EL TRABAJO

CHAQUETA	jacket yák-et
CHICO	little lít-tl
CIERRA/CERRAR	shut shót
COME/COMER	eat íit
¿CÓMO SE DICE?	How do you say? jáu du yu sei
¿CÓMO TE LLAMAS?	What is your name? juát iz yúr neim
COMPRA/COMPRAR	buy bái
COMPRENDE	understand ón-der-stand
CON	with uíd
CORRECTO	right ráit
CORTO	short shórt

PALABRAS Y FRASES COMUNES

¿CUÁNDO?	When? juén
¿CUÁNTO?	How much? jáu móch
¿CUÁNTOS?	How many? jáu mén-i
¡CUIDADO!	Look out! lúk áut
¡CUIDADO!	Watch out! uách aut
CUIDADOSAMENTE	carefully kér-fal-i
DAÑO	damage dám-ich
DE NADA.	You are welcome. yu ar uél-kom
DE NUEVO	again a-gén
DEBAJO	under ón-der

INGLES EN
EL TRABAJO

DEJAR	leave líiv
	quit kúit
DELGADO	thin zín
DEPARTAMENTO DE INMIGRACIÓN	Immigration Department im-a-grei-shon di-part-ment
DERECHA	right ráit
DESATA/DESATAR	untie on-tái
DESPUÉS	after eaf-ter
DÓLAR	dollar dó-lar
¿DÓNDE?	Where? juér
EMPIEZA/EMPEZAR	begin bi-guín
	start stáart

PALABRAS Y FRASES COMUNES

EMPUJA/EMPUJAR	push púsh
EN	in en on an
ENCIMA DE	over óu-ver
ENTRADA	entrance én-trans
ESCRIBE/ESCRIBIR	write ráit
ESE/ESA	that dát
ESO ES TODO.	That's all. dáts al
ESPERA AQUÍ.	Wait here. uéit jír
ESPESO	thick zík
¡ESTÁ BIEN!	That's good! dáts gúd

INGLES EN
EL TRABAJO

ESTE/ESTA	this dís
ESTOY ENFERMO(A) **NO PUEDO IR A** **TRABAJAR EL DÍA DE HOY.**	I'm sick I can't come to work today. aim sik ai kant cam tu uórk tu-dei
FILOSO	sharp sháarp
FIN	end end
FLACO	thin zín
FONDO	bottom bót-om
FRENTE	front frónt
FRÍO	cold kóuld
FUERA	out aut
GRACIAS	Thank you. zenk yu

PALABRAS Y FRASES COMUNES

GRANDE	big bíg
GRUESO	thick zík
¿HABLAS ESPAÑOL?	Do you speak Spanish? du yu spíik spanish
HALLA/HALLAR	find faind
HAZ/HACER	make meik
¿HAY ALGUN BAÑO QUE PUEDA USAR?	Is there a bathroom I may use? iz der a báaz-rum ai mei iúus
HERIDA	injury ín-cher-i
HOLA	hello jél-o
HOMBRE	man mán
HÁGALO ASÍ.	Do it like this. du et laik dis

INGLES EN
EL TRABAJO

HÚMEDO	moist
	móist
IGUAL	equal
	í-kual
INCORRECTO	wrong
	róng
INMIGRACIÓN	Border Patrol
	bór-der pa-tróul
INTERIOR	inside
	in-sáid
IR	go
	góu
IZQUIERDO	left
	léft
JALA/JALAR	pull
	púl
JUGO	juice
	dchúus
LARGO	long
	lóng
LENTO	slow
	slóu

PALABRAS Y FRASES COMUNES

LIMPIA ESTO	clean this up klín zis óp
LIMPIA/LIMPIAR	clean up klín óp
LIMPIO	clean klín
LLENA/LLENAR	fill fíl
LLENO	full fúl
LLEVAR/PUESTO	wear uér
LO SIENTO	sorry sóri
LOS DOS	both bóuz
MALO	bad bád
	wrong róng
ME	me mi

MEDIO	middle míd-l
MEJOR	better bét-er
MI NIÑO(A) ESTA ENFERMO.	My child is sick. mai cháild is sik
MÍRAME.	Watch me. uách mí
MUCHO	much mách
MUEVE/MOVER	move múuv
MUJER	woman úo-man
MUY BIEN.	Well done. uél dan
MUY	very véri
MÁS	more mór
MÍO	mine máin

PALABRAS Y FRASES COMUNES

NADA	nothing nó-zing
NECESITAR/NECESIDAD	need níid
NO	no nóu
NOMBRE	name néim
NUEVO	new niúu
NUNCA	never név-er
NÚMERO DE SEGURO SOCIAL	Social Security Number só-shial se-kiur-ti nám-ber
OTRA VEZ	again a-gén
OTRO	other ód-er
PAGA/PAGO/PAGAR	pay péi
PALABRA	word uórd

INGLES EN
EL TRABAJO

PARA	to stop tú stóp
PELIGROSO	dangerous déin-yer-os
PEQUEÑO	small smól
PERDÓN	sorry sóri
PESADO	heavy jév-i
POCO	a little a lít-tl
POCO HONDO	shallow shál-ou
PON/PONER	put pút
PONGA ATENCIÓN.	Pay attention. péi a-tén-shon
POR ENCIMA	over óu-ver
POR FAVOR ENSÉÑEME COMO HACER ESTO.	Please show me how to do this. pliz sho mi jau to du dis

PALABRAS Y FRASES COMUNES

POR FAVOR	please plíz
POR MEDIO DE	across a-krós
¿POR QUÉ?	Why? jiái
PRENDER	turn on tern an
PROFUNDO	deep díip
PRONTO	quick kúik
PRÓXIMO	next nékst
¿PUEDES ESCRIBIR?	Can you write? kan yu rait
¿PUEDES LEER?	Can you read? kan yu ríd
¿PUEDO SALIR TEMPRANO HOY?	May I leave early today? mei ai liv ér-li tu-dei
QUÉDESE/QUEDARSE	remain rí-mein

INGLES EN
EL TRABAJO

¿QUÉ?	What?
	júat
¿QUÉ QUIERE QUÉ HAGA?	What do you want me to do?
	juát du yu uánt mi tu du
¿QUIÉN?	Who?
	júu
¿QUIERES?	Do you want?
	du yu uánt
RÁPIDO	fast
	fáast
RÁPIDO	quick
	kúik
RECUERDA/RECORDAR	remember
	ri-mém-ber
SALIDA	exit
	ék-set
SALIR	leave
	líiv
SECO/SECAR	dry
	drái
SÍ	yes
	yés

PALABRAS Y FRASES COMUNES

SIENTO MUCHO LLEGAR TARDE.	I'm sorry I'm late. aim sá-ri aim leit
SÍGAME.	Follow me. fól-ou mi
SIN	without uíd-aut
SOBRE	on an
SÓLO	only óun-li
TARDE	late léit
TENGO QUE IR AL (DOCTOR, DENTISTA, HOSPITAL, CLINICA).	I have to go to the (doctor, dentist, hospital, clinic) ai jav tu gou tu da (dók-tor, dén-tist, jós-pi-tal, clí-nic)
TENGO HAMBRE.	I am hungry. ai am jón-gri
TERMINAR	end end
TIBIO	warm uórm

INGLES EN
EL TRABAJO

¿TIENES HAMBRE?	Are you hungry? aur yu ján-gri
TODO	all al
TOMA/TOMAR	takes, take téiks, téik
TRABAJO	work uórk
TRAE/TRAER	bring bríng
TRATA/TRATAR	try trái
TÚ	you yu
USA/USAR	use iúus
VACÍO	empty ém-ti
VE	go góu
VEN/VENIR	come kóm

PALABRAS Y FRASES COMUNES

¡VEN AQUÍ!	Come here! kóm jir
VIEJO	old oúld
YA ME VOY.	I'm leaving now. aim liv-ing nau
YO NECESITO / YO NO NECESITO ALMORZAR.	I need / do not need lunch. ai nid / du not nid lónch
YO NECESITO.	I need. ai nid
YO PUEDO HACER ESO.	I can do that. ai kan du dat
YO TENGO	I have ai jav
YO VENGE DE ...	I come from ... ai kóm fróm
YO QUIERO.	I want. ai juant
ÚLTIMO	last láast
ÚNICO	only óun-li

INGLES EN
EL TRABAJO

Parte II

CONSTRUCCIÓN

CONSTRUCCIÓN

CONSTRUCCIÓN	**CONSTRUCTION** kons-trók-shon
A NIVEL	level lév-l
ABANICO	fan fán
ACABAR	finish fín-ish
ACERO	steel stíil
AGUJERO	hole jóul
AIRE	air éer
ALAMBRE	wire uaír
ALBERCA	pool púul
ALZAR	lift líft
ANDAMIO	scaffold skáf-old
ÁNGULO	angle an-gl

INGLES EN
EL TRABAJO

ANTORCHA	torch tór-ch
ÁREA	area ér-i-a
ARENA	sand sánd
ARREGLAR	fix fíks
AYUDAR	help jélp
BALDE	bucket bók-et
BAÑERA	bathtub báaz-tob
BARRICADA	barricade ber-í-keid
BASURA	trash trásh
BLOQUE	block blóck
BORDE	edge éch

CONSTRUCCIÓN

BREA	tar táar
CABLE	cable kéi-bl
CADENA	chain chéin
CAER	drop dróp
CAJA	box bóks
CAJA DE HERRAMIENTAS	tool box túul bóks
CAMIÓN	truck trók
CANAL	channel chán-l
CARPETA	carpet kár-pet
CARPINTERO	carpenter kár-pen-tr
CASCAJO	gravel grá-vel

INGLES EN
EL TRABAJO

CEMENTO	cement
	sí-ment
CENTRO	center
	sént-er
CEPILLO	brush
	brósh
	plane
	pléin
CEPILLO DE PINTAR	paintbrush
	péint-brósh
CERRAR	lock
	lók
CHAPAPOTE	tar
	táar
CIERRA CON LLAVE	lock
	lók
CIMIENTOS	footings
	fút-ings
CINCEL	chisel
	chíz-l
CINTA DE MEDIR	tape measure
	teip mésh-ur

CONSTRUCCIÓN

CINTA	tape teip
CÍRCULO	circle sérk-l
CLAVO	nail néil
COLGAR	hang jáng
COMPONER	fix fíks
COMPRESOR DE AIRE	compressor kom-prés-or
CONECTAR	connect ko-nect
CORTAR	cut kót
CASCO PROTECTOR	hard hat jáard ját
CUADRADO	square skuér
CUARTO	room rúum

INGLES EN
EL TRABAJO

CUBETA	bucket bók-et
DEJAR	drop dróp
DERECHO	straight stréit
DESARMADOR	screwdriver skrúu-drai-ver
DESCARGAR	unload on-lóud
DESCONECTAR	disconnect dis-ko-nékt
DESIGUAL	uneven un-í-ven
DOBLAR	bend bénd
DRENAJE	drain dréin
	sewer su-er
EDIFICIO	building bíl-ding

CONSTRUCCIÓN

ELECTRICIDAD	electricity e-lec-trí-si-ti
EMPALMAR	splice splais
EMPAREJAR	grade greid
ENGRAPAR	staple stéi-pl
ENTRADA	gate géit
ENTRADA PARA CARROS	driveway drái-uéi
ESCALAR	climb up kláim ap
ESCALERA	ladder lád-er
ESCALERAS	stairs stéerz
ESCALÓN	step/stair stép/stéer
ESCOBA	broom brúum

INGLES EN
EL TRABAJO

ESCREN	screen skríin
ESQUINA	corner kór-nr
ESTIRAR	stretch stréch
ESTUCO	stucco stá-co
EXCAVA/EXCAVAR	dig dig
EXCUSADO	toilet tói-let
EXTENDER	extend eks-ténd
EXTERIOR	exterior eks-tí-ri-or
FILO	edge éch
FLOTA DE MANO	trowel tráu-el
FORMA	form fórm

CONSTRUCCIÓN

FORMANDO	framing fréi-ming
FORMAR	frame fréim
FOSA	trench tréntsh
FREGADERO	sink sínk
FUEGO	fire fáir
FUNDACIÓN	foundation faund-éi-shon
GABINETE	cabinet káb-i-net
GARLOPA	plane pléin
GATO	jack ják
GOMA PARA SELLAR	caulk kók
GORRA DE TRABAJO	hard hat jáard ját

INGLES EN
EL TRABAJO

GRAMPAS	staples stéi-plz
GRAPAS	staples stéi-plz
GRAPÓN	brace bréis
GRAVA	gravel grá-vel
GRIETA	crack krák
HACHA	axe áks
HERRAMIENTAS	tools túulz
HOJA DEL SERRUCHO ELÉCTRICO	sawblade sá-bleid
HOYO	hole jóul
INSULACIÓN	insulation in-sul-éi-shon
JALAR	haul jól

CONSTRUCCIÓN

JAMBA	jamb yám
JUNTAR	attach a-tách
LACA	lacquer lák-er
LADRILLO	brick brík
LEVANTAR	lift líft
LIMPIAR	clean klín
LINEA	line láin
LLANA	trowel tráu-el
LLAVE	faucet fá-set
LLAVE INGLESA	wrench rénch
LUZ	light láit

INGLES EN
EL TRABAJO

MADERA	lumber lóm-ber
	wood uúd
MALLA DE ACERO	mesh mesh
MANGO	handle ján-dl
MANGUERA	hose jóuz
MARCAR	mark márk
MARCO PARA PUERTA	jamb yám
MARTILLO	hammer jám-er
MARTILLO DE PRESIÓN DE AIRE	jackhammer ják-jam-er
MASILLA PARA RESENAR	putty pú-ti
MEDIDA	measurement méi-shur-ment

CONSTRUCCIÓN

MEDIR	measure mésh-ur
MEZCLA	mortar mór-tr
MEZCLAR	mix miks
MOLDURA	trim trím
MOSQUITERO	screen skríin
MUESCA	groove grúuv
MUESCA	notch nátch
NIVEL	level lév-l
OBRERO	worker uórk-er
ORGANIZA/ORGANIZAR	organize ór-ga-naiz
PALA	shovel shó-vl

INGLES EN
EL TRABAJO

PAPEL DE ENTAPIZAR	wallpaper uól-pei-per
PAPEL DE LIJA	sandpaper sánd-pei-per
PARALELO	parallel pár-a-lel
PARED	wall uól
PATIO	patio pá-ti-o
PAVIMENTO	pavement péiv-ment
PEGA/PEGAR	glue glúu
PEGAR	attach a-tách
PELIGRO	danger déin-yer
PERNO	bolt bóult
PICO	pick pík

CONSTRUCCIÓN

PIE(S)	foot/feet fút/fíit
PIEDRA	rock rók
PINTAR	paint péint
PINTOR	painter péint-er
PINTURA	paint péint
PINZAS	pliers plái-ers
PIPA	pipe páip
PISO	floor flór
PISO DE CEMENTO	slab slab
PLANOS	plans plánz
PLOMADA	plumb plóm

INGLES EN
EL TRABAJO

PLOMERO	plumber plóm-er
PLÁSTICO	plastic pláss-tik
POSTE	post póust
PRENSA DE SUJETAR	clamp klámp
PUERTA	door dór gate géit
PULGADA(S)	inch(es) inch(ez)
QUEMAR	burn bérn
QUITAR	remove ri-múv
RAMPA	ramp ráamp
RASPADOR	scraper scréi-per

CONSTRUCCIÓN

REGLA	level lév-l
RESISTOL	glue glúu
ROMPER	break breík
ROTO	broken bróu-ken
SECO	dry drái
SERRUCHO	saw sá
SIERRA DE CADENA	chain saw chéin sá
SIERRA PARA CORTAR METAL	hacksaw ják-saw
SUBTERRÁNEO	underground ón-der-graund
SUBIR	climb up kláim ap lift líft

INGLES EN
EL TRABAJO

SUCIO	dirty dért-i
SÓTANO	basement béis-ment
TAJAR	chop chóp
TALADRO	drill dríl
TECHO	ceiling sí-ling roof rúuf
TEJA	tile táil
TERMINAR	finish fín-ish
TERRAZA	deck dék
TIEMPO	time táim
¿TIENES EXPERIENCIA?	Do you have experience? du yu jav eks-pí-ri-ens

CONSTRUCCIÓN

TIERRA	dirt
	dért
TIZA	chalk
	chók
TORNILLO	screw
	skrúu
TRABAJADOR	worker
	uórk-er
TRABAJO	work
	uórk
TRIPLY	plywood
	plái-uúd
TUBA	pipe
	páip
UNIÓN	joint
	yóint
VENTANA	window
	uín-dou
VIDRIO	glass
	gláas
VIGA	rafter
	ráaf-ter

INGLES EN
EL TRABAJO

YESO   plaster
                        pláss-ter

ZANJA   ditch
                        dich

                        trench
                        tréntsh

Parte III

JARDINERÍA

JARDINERÍA

LANDSCAPING
land-skei-ping

ABONO	compost kóm-poust
	fertilizer fér-tilais-r
ACEITE	oil óil
AFLOJADOR DE TIERRA	roto-tiller róu-tou-til-er
AGUACATE	avocado a-vo-cá-do
AGUJERO	hole jóul
AIRE	wind uáind
ALAMBRE	wire uáir
ALBERCA	pool púul
APILAR	stack sták
APLICA/APLICAR	apply a-plái

71

INGLES EN
EL TRABAJO

ÁRBOL/ÁRBOLES	tree(s)
	tríi(z)
ARBUSTO	bush
	bósh
	shrub
	shrób
ARENA	sand
	sánd
ASFALTO	pavement
	péiv-ment
AZADÓN	hoe
	jóu
BABOSO	snail
	snéil
BANCO	bench
	bénch
BANQUETA	sidewalk
	sáid-uok
BASURA	trash
	trásh
BOLSA	bag
	bág

JARDINERÍA

BOLSA PARA BASURA	trashbag trásh-bag
BOMBA DE FUMIGAR	sprayer spréi-r
BOMBA	pump pómp
BOTE DE BASURA	trashcan trásh-kan
BOTÓN	bud búd
BROTE	bud búd
BULBO	bulb bólb
CARRETILLA	wheelbarrow juíil-ba-ro
CASCAJO	gravel grá-vl
CERCA/CERCO	fence féns
CEREZA	cherry cher-i

INGLES EN
EL TRABAJO

CÉSPED	grass gráas lawn lón
CHABACANO	apricot éi-pri-kat
CHARCA	pond pónd
CONCRETO	concrete kón-kriit
CORTADORA DE SACATE	lawn mower lón móu-er
CORTAR	chop chóp
CORTAR EL SACATE	mow the grass móu da gráas
CUBIERTA	deck dék
CULTIVAR	grow gró
DECLIVE	slope slóup

JARDINERÍA

DERRUMBE	erosion e-róu-shon
DESCARGA/DESCARGAR	unload ón-loud
DRENAJE	drainage dréin-ech
DURAZNO	peach píich
ELECTRICIDAD	electricity i-lek-trí-si-ti
EMPAPAR	soak sóuk
ENTRADA	gate géit
ENTRADA PARA CARROS	driveway dráiv-uéi
EROSIÓN	erosion e-róu-shon
ESCARCHA	frost fróst
ESCOBA	broom brúum

ESCOGER	pick pík
ESTACA	stake stéik
ESTACAR	stack sták
ESTIÉRCOL	manure ma-níu-r
ESTÁ SECO.	It is dry. it iz drai
EXCAVA/EXCAVAR	dig díg
FLORES	flowers fláu-erz
FLORIDO	flowerbed fláu-er-bed
FOLLAJE	foliage fol-ech
FORMAR	shape shéip
FRESA	strawberry stró-ber-i

JARDINERÍA

FRUTA	fruit
	frúut
FUMIGAR	spray
	spréi
GARAJE	garage
	gáa-rach
GAS	gas
	gás
GOTEAR	drip
	dríp
GUANTES	gloves
	glóvz
HACER EL JARDÍN	landscape
	lánd-skeip
HACHA	axe
	aks
HELADA	frost
	fróst
HERRAMIENTAS	tools
	túulz
HIEDRA	ivy
	ái-vi

INGLES EN
EL TRABAJO

HOJA	blade bléid
HOJAS	leaves lívz
HORMIGAS	ants antz
HOYO	hole jóul
INSECTICIDA	insecticide in-śk-ti-said
INSECTO	insect in-sekt
INSTALAR	install in-stól
INVERNADERO	greenhouse grín-jaus
IRRIGACIÓN	irrigation ir-ra-géi-shon
JARDÍN	garden gáar-dn
JARDINERO	gardener gáard-ner

JARDINERÍA

LADERA	slope slóup
LADRILLO	brick brík
LAVAR	wash uósh
LECHUGA	lettuce lét-is
LIMA	lime láim
LIMON	lime láim
LIMPIAR	clean up klín ap
LIMÓN	lemon lém-on
LISO	smooth smúud
LLUVIA	rain réin
LOCETA	tile táil

INGLES EN
EL TRABAJO

LUCES	lights
	láitz
MACETA	pot
	pót
MADERA	wood
	uúd
MADURO	ripe
	ráip
MALAS HIERBAS	weeds
	uiídz
MANDARINA	tangerine
	tán-yer-in
MANGO	handle
	ján-dl
MANGUERA	hose
	jóus
MANTENIMIENTO	maintenance
	méin-te-nans
MANZANA	apple
	áp-l
MECATE	rope
	róp

JARDINERÍA

MOJADO	wet uét
MOJAR DEMASIADO	soak sóuk
MOTOR	engine én-dyin
MÁQUINA	engine én-dyin
NARANJA	orange ór-anch
NECTARINA	nectarine nék-ta-rin
NO PONER DEMASIADO AGUA.	Don't overwater. dónt ov-ver-uó-ter
NURSERÍA	nursery nérs-er-i
PALA	shovel shá-vl
PALMA(S)	palm(s) páam(z)
PALO	pole pól

INGLES EN
EL TRABAJO

PARED DE RETENCIÓN	retaining wall ri-téin-ing uál
PARED	wall uól
PATIO	patio pá-ti-o yard yáard
PAVIMENTO	pavement péiv-ment
PEDAZOS DE CORTEZA	bark chips báark chipz
PIEDRA	stone stóun
PIEDRAS	rocks róks
PINO	pine páin
PIPA	pipe páip
PISCAR	pick pík

JARDINERÍA

PLANTA(S)	plant(s) pláant(z)
PLANTAR	grow gró
	plant pláant
PLATILLO	saucer sás-er
PODADOR	trimmers trím-mers
PODAR	prune prúun
	trim trím
PODER	power páu-er
PODOS	cuttings kót-ings
POSTE	post póust
POTENCIA	power páuer

PRADO	lawn lón
PREPARA/PREPARAR	prepare pri-pér
¿PUEDE PODAR?	Can you prune? kon yu prúun
QUEBRADO	broken bróu-quen
QUITAR	remove ri-múuv
QUÍMICA	chemical kém-e-kal
RAMA	limb lím
RASTRILLAR	rake réik
RASTRILLO	rake réik
RAÍZ/RAÍCES	roots rúut(z)
REGADERA	sprinkler sprínk-lr

JARDINERÍA

REGAR	water uó-tr
REMOVER	remove ri-múuv
REPARAR	repair ri-pér
REPONER	replace ri-pléis
RIBETEAR	edge éch
ROCIADOR	sprayer spréi-r
ROCIAR	spray spréi
ROSA	rose róus
SECAR LAS HIERBAS	weed uiíd
SEMILLA	seed síid
SENDA	path páaz

INGLES EN
EL TRABAJO

SERRUCHO DE MANO	handsaw jánd-sa
SETO	hedge jédch
SIERRA DE CADENA	chain saw chéin sá
SISTEMA DE RIEGO PARA JARDÍN	sprinkler system sprínk-lr sís-tem
SOGA	rope róp
SOL	sun són
SOMBRA	shade shéid
SOPLADOR	blower blóu-er
SUAVE	smooth smúud
SUBTERRÁNEO	underground ón-der-graund
SUBIR	climb up kláim ap

JARDINERÍA

TALLO	stem stém
TECHO	roof rúuf
TERRAZA	deck dék
TERRENO	land lánd
TIERRA ABONADA **PARA JARDÍN**	potting soil pót-ing sóil
TIERRA	dirt dért
TIRA/TIRAR	dump
TOBERA	nozzle ná-zl
TOMATE	tomato to-méi-tou
TORONJA	grapefruit gréip-fruut
TRABAJADOR	laborer léi-bor-er

INGLES EN
EL TRABAJO

TRACTOR	tractor trák-tor
TRANSPLANTAR	transplant tráns-plaant
TRONCO	stump stó-mp trunk trónk
VEGETAL	vegetable véch-ta-bl
VENENO	poison pói-son
VERDURAS	vegetables véch-tablz
VEREDA	path páaz
VIENTO	wind uáind
VÁLVULA	valve válv
YARDA	yard yáard

JARDINERÍA

ZANJA

ditch
dich

trench
tréntsh

Parte IV

SERVICIO DOMÉSTICO

SERVICIO DOMÉSTICO

SERVICIO DOMÉSTICO	HOUSEKEEPING jáus-kiip-ing
ABAJO	downstairs daun-stéerz
ABANICO	fan fán
ACERA	sidewalk sáid-uok
AGUA	water uó-tr
ALFOMBRA	carpet kár-pet rug róg
ALIMENTO	food fúud
ALMOHADA	pillow píl-ou
AMARIO PARA ROPA BLANCA	linen closet lín-en klás-et
ARENA	sand sánd
ARRIBA	upstairs áp-steerz

INGLES EN
EL TRABAJO

ASPIRADORA	vacuum
	vák-iuum
AZÚCAR	sugar
	chú-gar
BALDE	bucket
	bók-et
BANDEJA	tray
	trei
BAÑERA	bathtub
	baz-tób
BAÑO	bathroom
	baz-rúum
	restroom
	rest-rúum
BARBACOA	barbecue
	bár-bi-kiu
BARRE/BARRER	sweep
	suíip
BASURA	trash
	trásh
BLANQUEAR	bleach
	bleích

SERVICIO DOMÉSTICO

BOLSA PARA BASURA	trashbag trásh bag
BOLSA PARA ASPIRADORA	vacuum bag vák-iuum bág
BOMBILLA	light bulb láit búlb
BOTE DE BASURA	trashcan trash-kan
BOTÓN	button bót-n
BURRO	ironing board ái-rn-ing bórd
CACEROLAS	pans pánz
CAFÉ	coffee káf-i
CAJA	box bóks
CAJÓN	drawer dró-er
CALCETÍN	socks soks

INGLES EN
EL TRABAJO

CALIENTE	hot
	ját
CAMA	bed
	bed
CAMISA	shirt
	shért
CARPETA	carpet
	kár-pet
CASA	house
	jáus
CENICERO	ashtray
	ásh-trei
CENIZA	ashes
	a-shz
CEPILLO	brush
	brósh
CERA	wax
	uáks
CERILLOS	matches
	mách-es
CERRADURA	lock
	lók

SERVICIO DOMÉSTICO

CERRAR CON LLAVE	lock lók
CESTO DE ROPA	hamper jám-per
CHAMPÚ	shampoo sham-púu
CHIMENEA	fireplace fáir-pleis
CLORO	bleach bleích
COBIJA	blanket bleing-ket
COCINA	kitchen kít-chen
COLCHA	bedspread béd-spred
COLCHÓN	mattress mat-res
COLGAR	hang jáng
COMEDOR	dining room dai-ning rúum

INGLES EN
EL TRABAJO

COMPRAS	shopping shóp-ing
CONGELADOR	freezer fríi-ser
CORTINAS	curtains kér-tinz
COSER	sew sú
CRIADA	maid méid
CUADRO	picture pík-chur
CUARTO	room rúum
CUARTO DE FAMÎLIA	family room fám-i-li rúum
CUARTO DE HUÉSPED	guest room guést rúum
CUARTO DE LAVANDERÍA	laundry room lón-dri rúum
CUBETA	bucket bók-et

SERVICIO DOMÉSTICO

CUBIERTOS	silverware síl-ver-uer
CUBO DE HIELO	ice bucket áis bók-et
CUBRIR	cover kó-ver
CUCHARA	spoon spúun
CUCHILLO	knife náif
CUNA	crib crib
DELANTAL	apron éi-pron
DETERGENTE	detergent de-tér-gent
DOBLAR	fold fóuld
DORMIDO	asleep a-slíip
DUCHA	shower sháu-er

INGLES EN
EL TRABAJO

EMPAPAR	soak sóuk
ENCERAR	wax uáks
ENJUAGA/ENJUAGAR	rinse ríns
ESCALERA	ladder lád-er
ESCALERAS	stairs stéerz
ESCOBA	broom brúum
ESCRITORIO	desk désk
ESCURREPLATOS/ **ESCURRIDOR**	drainboard dréin-bord
ESPEJO	mirror mír-or
ESPONJA	sponge spónch
ESTANTE	shelf shélf

SERVICIO DOMÉSTICO

ESTUFA	stove stóuv
EXCUSADO	toilet tói-let
FOCO	light bulb láit búlb
FREGADERO	sink sínk
FREGAR	scrub skrób
FRÍO	cold cóuld
FUEGO	fire fáir
FUMAR	smoke smóuk
FUNDA	pillowcase píl-ou-keis
GABINETES	cupboards kó-bordz
GANCHO	hanger jáng-er

INGLES EN
EL TRABAJO

GARAJE	garage gáa-rach
GUANTES	gloves glóvz
HELADOR	freezer fríi-ser
HERRAMIENTAS	tools túulz
HIELO	ice áis
HILO	thread zréd
HORNO	oven ó-ven
HUELLAS	fingerprints fín-guer-prentz
HUÉSPEDES	guests guésts
JABÓN	soap sóup
JUGUETE(S)	toy(s) toi(z)

SERVICIO DOMÉSTICO

LATA	can kán
LAVADORA	washing machine uósh-ing má-chiin
LAVANDERÍA	laundry lón-dri
LAVAPLATOS	dishwasher dish-uósh-er
LAVAR	wash uósh
LECHE	milk mílk
LEÑA	firewood fáir-uúd
LEVANTAR LA MESA	clear the table klíir de tei-bol
LIBRO	book búk
LIMPIA/LIMPIAR	clean klíin
LIMPIADORA	cleaner klíin-er

LLAVE	faucet fó-set
LLAVE	key kíi
LUMBRE	flame fléim
LUSTRE/LUSTRAR	polish pól-ish
LUZ	light láit
LÁMPARA	lamp lámp
LINEA DE ROPA	clothes line clóuzs lain
MADERA	wood uúd
MALETA	suitcase siúut-keis
MANCHA	spot, stain spót, stéin
MANDADO	groceries gróu-sr-iz

SERVICIO DOMÉSTICO

MANDIL	apron éi-pron
MAPEAR	mop máp
MECHERO	burner bérn-er
MERCADO	market máar-ket
MESA	table téi-bl
MICROHONDA	microwave mái-kro-ueiv
MOSTRADOR	counter káun-ter
MUEBLES	furniture fór-ni-chur
OFICINA	office áf-is
OLLAS	pots pótz
ORDENADO	neat níit

INGLES EN
EL TRABAJO

PANTALLA	lampshade lámp-sheid
PANTALONES	pants pántz
PAÑAL	diaper dai-per
PAPEL	paper péi-per
PAPEL HIGIÉNICO	toilet paper tói-let péi-per
PARED	wall uól
PASILLO	hallway jól-uei
PERIÓDICO	newspaper niúuz-pei-per
PIMIENTA	pepper pép-er
PISO	floor flór
PLANCHA	iron ái-rn

SERVICIO DOMÉSTICO

PLATOS	dishes, plates
	dísh-ez, pleitz
POLVO	dust
	dóst
PONER LA MESA	set the table
	sét da téi-bl
PORTERO	janitor
	yán-et-or
PUERTA	door
	dór
PULIR	polish
	pól-ish
QUEMADOR	burner
	bérn-er
RADIO	radio
	réi-di-o
RASCAR	scrape
	scréip
RASPAR	scrape
	scréip
RECOGEDOR	dustpan
	dóst-pan

RECÁMARA	bedroom bed-rúum
REFRIGERADOR	refrigerator ri-frí-ya-rei-tor
REMIENDA/REMENDAR	mend ménd
REPISA	shelf shélf
RESTREGAR	scrub skrób
REVISTA	magazine mea-ga-zín
ROPA BLANCA	linen lín-en
ROPA	clothes clóuzs
ROPA INTERIOR	underwear ón-der-uer
ROPERO	closet klá-set
SACUDIR	dust dóst

SERVICIO DOMÉSTICO

SACUDIR	shake shéik
SAL	salt sólt
SALA	living room lív-ing rúum
SARTENES	pans pánz
SECADOR	dryer drái-er
SECAR	dry drái
SERVILLETAS	napkins náp-kins
SILLON	couch káuch
SOBRECAMA	bedspread béd-spred
SOFÁ	couch káuch
SUCIO	dirty dér-ti

INGLES EN
EL TRABAJO

SÁBANAS	sheets shíitz
TABLA DE PLANCHAR	ironing board ái-rn-ing bórd
TAPADERA	lid líd
TAPAR	cover kó-ver
TAZA	cup ióp
TEJA	tile táil
TELEVISIÓN	television tel-e-vísh-on
TELÉFONO	telephone tél-e-foun
TENDER LA CAMA	make the bed méik da bed
TENEDOR	fork fórk
TETERO	baby bottle béi-bi bot-tl

SERVICIO DOMÉSTICO

TIBIO	warm uórm
TIJERAS	scissors sís-ers
TOALLA DE PAPEL	paper towel péi-per táu-el
TOALLAS	towels táu-elz
TOCADOR	dresser drés-er
TOSTADOR	toaster tóust-er
TRABAJO	work uórk
TRAJE	suit siúut
TRAPEADOR	mop máp
TRAPEAR	mop máp
TRAPO	rag rág

INGLES EN
EL TRABAJO

TRASTES	dishes, plates
	dísh-ez, pleitz
UNIFORME	uniform
	iúu-ni-form
VACIAR	empty
	ém-ti
VASIJA	bowl
	bául
VASO	glass
	gláas
VENENO	poison
	pói-sn
VESTÍBULO	lobby
	lób-i
VIDRIO	glass
	gláas
ZAPATOS	shoes
	shúuz

Parte V

CUADROS

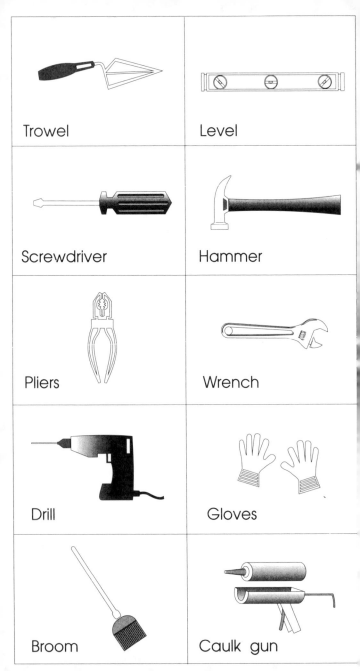

Trowel	Level
Screwdriver	Hammer
Pliers	Wrench
Drill	Gloves
Broom	Caulk gun

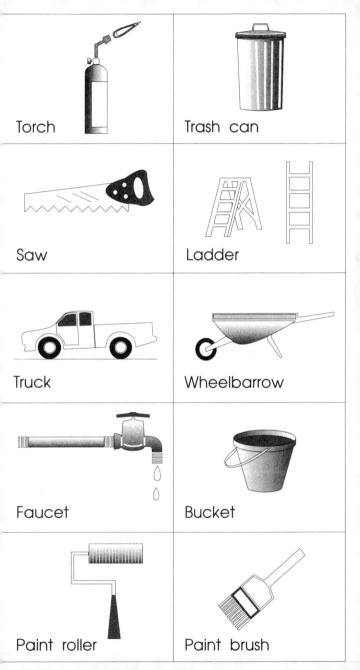

Torch	Trash can
Saw	Ladder
Truck	Wheelbarrow
Faucet	Bucket
Paint roller	Paint brush

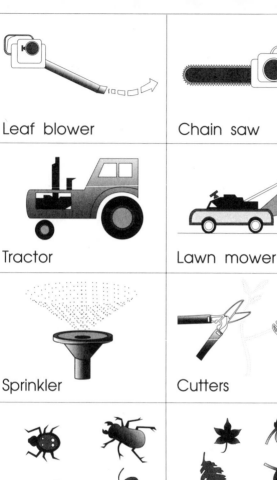

Leaf blower	Chain saw
Tractor	Lawn mower
Sprinkler	Cutters
Insects	Leaves
Poison	Sprayer

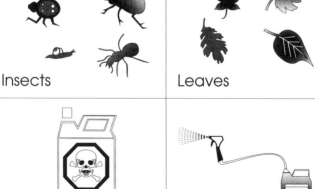

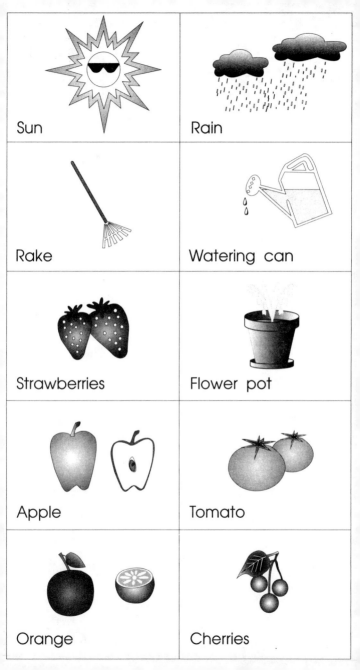

Sun

Rain

Rake

Watering can

Strawberries

Flower pot

Apple

Tomato

Orange

Cherries

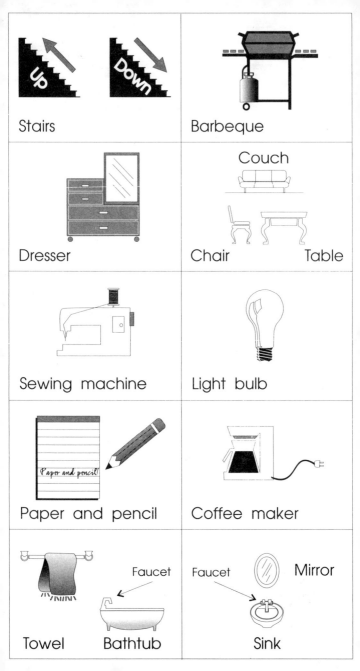

Stairs	Barbeque
Dresser	Couch Chair　　Table
Sewing machine	Light bulb
Paper and pencil	Coffee maker
Towel　　Bathtub	Sink

Faucet

Faucet　　Mirror